From Darkness To Light

From Darkness To Light

by
Jeffrey C. Fenholt

Harrison House
Tulsa, Oklahoma

Unless otherwise indicated, all Scripture quotations are taken from the *King James Version* of the Bible.

2nd Printing
Over 160,000 in Print

From Darkness To Light
ISBN 0-89274-730-7
Copyright © 1994 by Jeffrey C. Fenholt
P.O. Box 5000-301
Upland, California 91786

Published by Harrison House, Inc.
P.O. Box 35035
Tulsa, Oklahoma 74153

Foreword

By Paul F. Crouch

He brought them out of darkness and the shadow of death, and brake their bands in sunder (Psalms 107:14)

Jeff Fenholt appeared on the scene as one of Broadway's brightest new stars. His success in the lead role of the hit musical, Jesus Christ Superstar, launched him into the limelight of the music world. Talent, fame, fortune — he seemed to have it all; but, there was something desperately missing in his life that could not be satisfied with all of his possessions and abilities. The pages that follow tell the wonderful story of Jeff's encounter with the *real* Jesus Christ, and how he was gloriously saved and delivered through the power of God. Interestingly, Jeff was approached by the producers of the recently revived version of Jesus Christ Superstar, and was asked if he would consider playing his former role again. He completely turned down their offer. When Jeff came to Jesus his life was radically changed, and he now only sings praises that glorify the Lord.

Jeff and his wife Reeni have been a special blessing to the TBN network where they regularly appear on the "Praise the Lord" program. They are the hosts of their own television series, "Highway To Heaven," which is also aired on the TBN network. In recent years, Jeff has been a part of TBN's Russian evangelistic crusades where audiences remembered him from his former days as Jesus Christ Superstar. the impact was overwhelming as they heard Jeff's testimony and saw the change that God has brought about in his life. Jeff's ministry in Russia continues as his television program is now airing on Channel 40 in St. Petersburg, Russia and on Channel 3 in Moscow.

God has gifted Jeff with a wonderful vocal talent that has blessed countless millions around the world. Jeff's ministry touches the lives of young and old alike, and he has had a special impact in reaching young people who are involved in the world of drugs and rock 'n roll. Many people have come to know Christ as Savior as he has shared his amazing testimony.

From Darkness to Light, is a powerful story of God's saving grace. After you've read it, we would encourage you to use this book as a witnessing tool, and maybe pass it along to someone who needs to know Jesus.

We salute Jeff and Reeni, and pray that many more precious lives will be won for the Kingdom of God through their ministry.

Paul F. Crouch, President
Trinity Broadcasting Network

Contents

Dedication

This book is dedicated to Maureen Hope Marie.

A Word From the Author

This book has been written with the hope of reaching the lost. I am certain that many brothers and sisters in Christ will also find it an inspiration in their continuing walk with the Lord.

In order to protect those written about in the book who are not yet saved, many names have been purposefully omitted. Also in order to condense this writing, many events that happened in lengthy chronological order have been condensed.

It is my desire that you will be uplifted as you read this book, this testimonial.

1
Childhood and Adolescence

I grew up tough. My earliest recollection is that of being beaten as a child. I recall having pillows placed over my head and being beaten mercilessly. There were times when I would be thrown down the stairs, kicked, slapped and scratched deep in my flesh.

Many times I found myself frustrated beyond belief. One of those instances occurred in the middle of the night when, without warning, a pitcher of ice water was poured over me while I was in bed. Needless to say, I was filled with hatred.

My parents divorced when I was in grade school, and my father was never there for me in any way, shape or form.

I hit the streets at an early age and began doing the usual things that rebellious youngsters do: drinking beer, smoking cigarettes, cursing, getting into fist fights. Then I graduated to stealing cars, breaking and entering, etc.

One day, when I was twelve years old, I saw a police paddy wagon pull up to my house. Two officers dressed in black uniforms got out and walked up to the door. They knocked on the door and I began wondering if it was me they were looking for, and, if so, what I had done to get into trouble.

When I came down the stairs, one of the police officers pointed to me and said, "Is that the boy?"

Much to my surprise I heard my mother say, "Yes, that's the one."

One of the officers pulled me down the stairs, dragged me out the door, threw me down in the grass and told me to lie face down.

"You are under arrest," he said.

I was taken to juvenile detention hall where I quickly learned that my mother had filed charges against me for incorrigibility. It was rough being in detention. There were different cliques, different factions of young men in that place. Some had long hair, some had greased hair, some had tattoos and no teeth; and then there was me. I was in my own space. And, I was scared to death!

Several of the young men began to tell me about how their mothers were working feverishly with attorneys trying to get them out of jail. All I could think of was the fact that my mother was the one who had put me there.

I was taken to see a psychiatrist. After a lengthy psychoanalysis, the psychiatrist filed this report: "This young man, Jeffrey Craig Fenholt, is unnatural. There is absolutely no love in him for anyone or anything." (I can't imagine why there was no love in me, can you?)

I believe the youth of today are paying for the sins of their parents. The Word of God tells us that God visits the generations that follow the sins of the fathers and reaches out to turn them to repentance. It is only through the blood of Jesus that the demonic chain of events caused by sin can be broken.

> The Lord is longsuffering, and of great mercy, forgiving iniquity and transgression, and by no means clearing the guilty, visiting the iniquity of the fathers upon the children unto the third and fourth generation.
>
> Numbers 14:18

> Thou shalt not bow down thyself unto them, nor serve them: for I the Lord thy God am a jealous God, visiting the iniquity of the fathers upon the children unto the third and fourth generation of them that hate me.
>
> Deuteronomy 5:9

Then came the day I was to face my accuser and a judge. When I began hearing what a horrible young man I was, I started yelling and trying to defend myself. I told the judge: "I'm a victim of circumstance. I'm a product of my environment. I'm not the one who's rotten here; it's my home life that's rotten. I'm beaten and kicked and verbally abused. I have nowhere to go after school, no place to sleep at night. There's no place where I am safe. All I want is to be on the streets. I'm the one who needs to be protected."

The judge looked me straight in the eye and in a very hardened manner spoke to me: "Son, if you are a delinquent, then we need to protect society from you. And if, in fact, your home life is as terrible as you say it is, then we need to protect you from it. But, unfortunately, either way you lose!"

He then sentenced me to juvenile hall and later to what was known as the boys' industrial school.

That night I cried out, "If there is a God in heaven, You've got to help me."

The next day when I woke up I was still in jail, the warden was still alive, my mother had pressed charges against me and everything was exactly the same as it had been before I prayed. So I decided there was no God because He didn't answer my prayer. I had absolutely no understanding of God, and I definitely had no understanding of Who Jesus is.

And I will sow her unto me in the earth; and I will have mercy upon her that had not obtained mercy; and I will say to them which were not my people, Thou art my people; and they shall say, Thou art my God.

Hosea 2:23

Later, as I was walking in the halls a very large middle-aged man came over to me and said, "Son, you don't belong here. You're not like these other boys."

I was taken to an office with this man. There I was told that he was a "minister" and that he was willing to sign me over to his care. I was informed that he would become my legal guardian in order to see me released from jail. I figured, *Why not?*

I got in the car with this man and drove to the rectory adjoining his church, a part of one of the mainstream denominations. I soon learned that this man was not married and that he lived alone in the building.

Later that evening he came to me and in a very effeminate voice said, "Son, you've been through a tremendously stressful situation. You're very tense and uptight. I want to relax you." Then he asked me to strip down so he could give me a back rub. Need I say more? It was obvious there was something wrong with the man.

Having a form of godliness, but denying the power thereof: from such turn away.

2 Timothy 3:5

God's Word says in 1 John 4:19, **We love him, because he first loved us.** In Romans 5:8 we read, **But God commendeth his love toward us, in that, while we were yet sinners, Christ died for us.**

Christ died on the cross for me while I was still a sinner. More than that, as I look back on my life, I know that the Lord was watching over and protecting me, even during those horrible times when I was a young child. For example, He saw to it that the man I went to live with was never successful in molesting me. However, he did make my life miserable for a while.

Within several weeks of that experience, my mother signed the papers allowing me to return home to live with her. At that point she told me, "From now on you are going to do everything I tell you. When I say jump, you are going to ask how high. If I have any problem with you, all I have to do is pick up the telephone and call the police, and you're back in jail!"

Several times I found myself back in jail by my mother's hand. What a wonderful and secure way to grow up. Naturally, bitterness and hatred continued to fill my heart.

I began noticing other young people, together with their parents, out having fun, stopping at the Dairy Queen or relaxing in the park. I would resent these youngsters for having a good family who loved them and took care of them.

> Train up a child in the way he should go: and when
> he is old, he will not depart from it.
>
> Proverbs 22:6

I was trained to be violent, and violence was what I wanted to express.

I decided to get involved in rock and roll music, so I organized my first rock group when I was twelve years old. Immediately we were hired to play at teen dances. We furnished our group with the best public address system money could buy. But we didn't buy it; we stole it from a church. You could say that the church gave us our start.

For the next several years I continued to rock, when I was not in trouble or in jail. By the time I was fifteen years old, I had made my first hit record with a group called "The Fifth Order." We hit the Top 40 charts and were the most popular rock group and had the number one record throughout the Midwest. The song was called "Goin' Too Far," which pretty much expressed my feelings about the people in authority around me. A second hit record followed entitled "1000 Devils."

I was also singing the blues. However, I wanted violence to be a part of my music, so I added a heavy rock beat to the blues vocals and came up with a mixture that just couldn't miss.

The crowds who came to hear us play grew to as many as three or four thousand young people a night. I began touring, playing six or seven nights a week during the summer and four nights a week during the school year.

I rented an apartment, moved out of my mother's house and began living my own life, all at age sixteen. I figured I had it made. I was making up to a thousand dollars a week, more money than my neighborhood principal earned! I was able to hang out with any of the young girls I chose. I was living among the most rebellious teenagers in the area. We were growing our hair long and wearing blue jeans, boots and leathers. We were cursing, spitting, calling people names, pulling dirty pranks, smoking pot, dropping pills, playing rock and roll music, drawing large crowds and making "big bucks." I was completely independent of any higher authority and influence — at least, so I thought.

> **If I say, Surely the darkness shall cover me; even the night shall be light about me.**
>
> **Yea, the darkness hideth not from thee; but the night shineth as the day: the darkness and the light are both alike to thee.**
>
> **Psalm 139:11,12**

One night while I was "rockin' and rollin'," I looked out into the audience and saw the most beautiful young lady I had ever laid eyes on. I asked around and learned that she lived in the wealthiest part of that city. Her name was Maureen Hope Marie McFadden. She was an Irish Catholic girl who went to a private school run by convent nuns. Apparently she and her girlfriends had decided to rebel and had come out to view a hard rock concert. I was immediately smitten by her and wanted to find some way to meet her and to begin a relationship with her. That process ended up taking two or three months. Eventually I was able to call and ask her for a date. Much to my surprise, she accepted.

The night came for us to go out. However, instead of showing up at her house as planned, I wound up getting drunk, so I never made it. I did call her later and apologized over and over, telling her some "big story." She agreed to give me one more chance.

The next time we had a date I made sure I showed up. I met her father, and quite frankly he almost died when I pulled up in my convertible with my long hair and my heavy rock look!

Maureen, or Reeni as her friends called her, lived in an enormous house and was the seventh child of a deeply religious family. Her father owned his own company and was one of the most successful business-men in that area. I had never seen anything like the McFaddens in my life. I didn't know that there were such families in existence. I thought they had gone out with Donna Reed, the Cleavers and Ozzie and Harriet — as I had been led to believe from my own experience throughout my tormented childhood.

I thought, *This is incredible. Not only is Reeni the most beautiful young lady I have ever seen, but her family is rich and loving. She's everything I want in a girl.*

Isn't it strange how, no matter how rotten a person may be, deep in his heart he wants the best, not the worst?

I began sharing with Reeni about my horrible life and I noticed that she seemed to be quite intrigued with me — as I was with her. Just as I was impressed by her wealth and good family life, Reeni was concerned about my rotten family life and personal situation. So we dated on and off from that point on.

My involvement with drugs, alcohol, sex, rock and roll music and violence continued throughout high school. When I was seventeen years old a violent incident occurred.

I was with two of my friends late one night. We had been drinking heavily and were looking for trouble. When we arrived at a pizza hangout, we were told that a very large teenager had beaten up one of our friends and was sitting inside the establishment.

This young man was approximately six feet four inches tall, and I would guess that he weighed well over two hundred pounds. Obviously he was too large for any one of us to go after, so we decided to jump him as a group.

When he left the pizza parlor on foot with a friend, we followed him by car into the darkness. As he turned down a rather quiet residential street, the three of us jumped out and attacked him. When we began beating him, the young man with him ran off into the night.

While he was on his hands and knees begging for help after we had severely beaten him, I ran toward him and kicked him directly in the face. I was wearing heavy work boots with steel toes. I heard a crack and saw blood spatter all over his face as he fell over backwards. As we ran from the yard of the house in front of which he was lying, we saw some adults come running out the door to his aid.

The next night I was arrested at a hamburger stand for curfew violation. While I was arguing with the police about my arrest, one officer looked at me and said, "We're doing this for your own good. Last night some punks attacked a young man, not too far from here, and now he's in a coma with a brain concussion. It's likely that he will die."

My friends and I had no regret or guilt for our crime. We were only concerned with not getting caught.

Thankfully, the young man recovered. Several months later I ran into him at a department store and was terrified that he would identify me to the police. He looked right at me and evidently did not recognize me. I was tremendously relieved. The only thing I can figure is that his beating was so severe he had a loss of memory. Still, I was not sorry, just filled with hate.

After graduation I began to consider my life and decided that I needed to make some serious decisions about my future. I realized that entertainers such as heavy metal rock and rollers are not the people who control the wealth in the United States of America; it is the businessmen. Reeni's father, for instance, worked in a nice office and lived in a manner that I had never seen or experienced.

I decided that I was going to give up rock and roll long enough to get through college so I would have something to fall back on later in life. I was extremely ambitious. I wanted wealth, success, a big home and a mega career. In short, I wanted everything the world had to offer, and I decided that the way to get it was through education, perseverance and aggressive behavior.

But rather seek ye the kingdom of God; and all these things shall be added unto you.

Luke 12:31

I decided to attain a college degree in music and marketing. When I was finished "rocking out" I would work for or start my own record company.

Young Jeff

Reeni

2
On the Road

I auditioned for and received a voice scholarship to Ohio State University. There I was placed in the men's glee club. Talk about trying to fit a square peg into a round hole!

During my first year of college, I decided to go out with a friend to a rock and roll concert in a neighboring town. While we were there, a fight erupted. We were attacked by a group of about ten young thugs. Apparently they thought we were flirting with their girlfriends. However, I seem to recall that it was the other way around.

My friend wound up in the hospital where he nearly died. He had a bruise on his brain and internal bleeding. I was arrested, thrown into the county jail, and charged with inciting a riot, assault and battery, resisting arrest and assaulting a police officer. My friends put their money together to get me out. I skipped bail and never went back.

At this point I realized that I was not going to succeed in my quest for a decent college life. I was a "headbanger," deeply devoted to hardcore music and — as I referred to myself — "a child of darkness."

Shortly thereafter I left the university for summer vacation and decided to go on tour with a rock group. My plan was to tour with them during the summer and earn a good deal of money so as not to have to rely on a music scholarship, if and when I decided to complete college.

Shortly after leaving on tour, I was offered a recording contract by CBS records. I had written and recorded a few songs, submitted them to CBS and been immediately signed. God had given me a tremendous gift for music. I was convinced that I was the best rock and roll singer in the world.

During my time on the road I began to meet different members of satanic groups. I started delving into the occult and attending parties where satanic rituals such as the drinking of blood were performed.

When I arrived on the West Coast, I was given one night off while in San Diego, California. I didn't want to have anything to do with the other people on the tour. I wanted to go down to the X-rated part of town, pick up some rude young lady, get drunk, smoke some pot, drop some pills and party.

As I was walking down the street, some guy came up to me. He was probably about nineteen or twenty years old. He looked me straight in the eye. I looked back at him and thought, *Who is this Bozo?*

He was wearing a sport coat, a pair of slacks and brogue shoes. He had a short "strange" haircut that would not come into fashion for at least another ten years. He asked me my name and I said, "It's none of your business."

"I want to know," he persisted. "What's your name?"

"Puddintane." I answered. "Now get out of my face, and don't follow me."

But he continued following me saying, "I want to talk to you."

Finally I turned around and asked him, "What have you got to say?"

His response was: "For God so loved you that He gave His only begotten Son, Jesus. If you believe in Him, you will not perish but will have eternal life."

I looked at him and said, "You're crazy. God didn't give His Son for me; Jesus died for nobody. Let me tell you about Jesus. If you want to believe that Jesus is God, well, that's fine, then Jesus is God. But He came down here to show us how to live. He posed for a few paintings holding sheep on His shoulders so everybody would know that He was real nice and mild. He had long hair and was a radical. He was so cool that the political leaders hung Him on a cross and killed Him. Then apparently He went to heaven. Now if we live like Him, we can go to heaven. If we don't live like Him, we are going to hell. I'm not going to be able to live like Him 'cause I'm a headbanger, so I'm going to hell. But I don't care, man, 'cause that's where my friends are, and when I get there we're going to party hearty!"

And death and hell were cast into the lake of fire. This is the second death.

And whosoever was not found written in the book of life was cast into the lake of fire.

Revelation 20:14,15

The guy looked at me and said, "No, you're wrong. Jesus loves you. Jesus is the way, the truth and the life.

No one goes to heaven except through Him. You need to be born again. You need to receive Jesus as your Lord and Savior and be filled with His power to overcome; then you will see eternal life."

If he had done anything other than quote Scripture to me, I guarantee you that I would have made a fool of him. But no matter what I said or how I tried to counter what he was presenting to me, I would run out of questions and answers because it is impossible to strike down God's Word, as the Lord says:

> So shall my word be that goeth forth out of my mouth: it shall not return unto me void, but it shall accomplish that which I please, and it shall prosper in the thing whereto I sent it.
>
> **Isaiah 55:11**

I became so intrigued with Jesus through this young man's conversation with me that I told him I would get on a bus and go hear more about Him. We wound up at a revival approximately twenty miles from town. There were all kinds of people in that place — drunks, prostitutes, street people, businessmen, grandmothers and children. They were dancing, screaming and shouting.

I remember there was one very pretty young lady down near the front row, so of course I went down and sat beside her. She looked at me and the next thing I knew, she started crying and sobbing and raising her hands. I thought, *What's the matter with her? This girl is really shook up, she's really upset.*

So I leaned over and tapped her on the shoulder and said, "Hey, baby, I don't know what's going on with you, but whatever it is, chill out. As soon as this thing is over, I'll take you out, we'll get drunk and party."

I had never heard of anybody crying out to the Lord. I had never heard of the joy of the Spirit. I didn't know anything about God.

At the end of the service there was what these people called an altar call. The leader asked that everybody who wanted to receive Jesus come forward. Many people got up and went down to the front. I didn't respond so I figured: *Good, now this thing's over so I can get back on their bus and leave.*

But that wasn't the case. The preacher began looking at me and yelling that there were others in the audience who needed to be saved. Then he walked around and said, "There are sinners here who have not repented and come to the Lord." Finally, he pointed to me and said, "Young man, you are a sinner!"

I looked back at him and answered, "Yeah? What's your first clue?"

Then he started pretending that he was preaching to the whole crowd but he kept looking at me all the time. After fifteen or twenty minutes of his trying to get "others" to come forward and receive Jesus, I realized that he was going to keep on pounding away until I did something. So I decided to go forward and receive Jesus in front of all those morons because that preacher wasn't going to shut up until I did. Then I could get on the bus and get out of there.

So I stood up. When I did, the crowd went crazy. Everybody started cheering.

There I was in my leathers, my boots, my blue jean shirt, with ripped off sleeves and patches all over me. Gold chains and jewelry were hanging all over my body. My hair was halfway down to my waist and was streaked blond and white. I stood about five feet eleven inches tall, weighed about 128 pounds and had black circles under my eyes from drugs and lack of sleep. I must have been some kind of sight for those Christians!

They cheered as I walked down the aisle. I remember looking around and thinking, *What a bunch of maroons.*

When I got to the altar, I made one mistake. I looked up at the ceiling and said a little prayer. I prayed, "Jesus, if You're real, show me."

The next thing I knew, a sensation the likes of which I had never known came over me. I felt what I would later learn to be the power of the Holy Spirit fall on me. I began to feel my hardened heart melting away.

Then will I sprinkle clean water upon you, and ye shall be clean: from all your filthiness, and from all your idols, will I cleanse you.

A new heart also will I give you, and a new spirit will I put within you: and I will take away the stony heart out of your flesh, and I will give you a heart of flesh.

Ezekiel 36:25,26

A surge of emotions swept over me and I went down on my knees and struggled to hold back the tears. All at once it was as if my eyes had been unscaled and I knew that there is a God and that Jesus is Lord. Under my breath I said, "Jesus, Jesus, You are real!"

I looked up at that preacher and said, "I'm going to accept Jesus as my Lord and Savior right now."

The preacher looked at me and replied, "Son, stand up."

When I stood up, he told me, "If you think that you're going to receive Jesus in my church looking like that, you've got another thing coming."

I was shocked.

"What do you mean?" I asked.

"Look at you," he answered. "I know who you are. I've spoken to the counselors who came with you on the bus."

Then he yelled to the audience, "This is the lead singer of that rock group that will be down at the auditorium tomorrow night leading our young people to hell!"

He turned to me and ordered, "Cut your hair. Put on some decent clothes. Come back here in a week and maybe we'll let you receive Jesus."

"What are you talking about, man?" I asked. "What's wrong with the way I'm dressed?"

"Look at you. You have hair halfway down your back. You look like a girl."

Suddenly all that feeling about God and Jesus, all the emotion that had hit me through the power of the Holy Ghost just moments before, was gone. I was cold. I looked that preacher right in the eye and told him, "You think I look like a girl, man? Well, if I look like a girl to you, then you must be hanging around with some very ugly women!"

Then I turned to the audience and cussed them out. I was thrown out of the church. I was forced to hitchhike back to San Diego.

For *whosoever* shall call upon the name of the Lord shall be saved.

Romans 10:13

I spoke to God several times that night. I told Him, "I don't fit in with Your people. They're running some kind of country club and I don't belong. I guess Your Church is just for wealthy people who come from good backgrounds and dress well. I just don't fit in with that crowd."

I didn't go back to the X-rated part of town. Instead I returned to my hotel room which overlooked the ocean at Mission Bay. I left all the lights off, fell to my knees and cried out, "God, help me. I felt You tonight, but there's no way I could ever serve You because I don't fit in. There's nothing I can give You but my talent. You created this voice in me, and now I give it back to You."

Be ye mindful always of his covenant; the word which he commanded to a thousand generations.

1 Chronicles 16:15

Delight thyself also in the Lord; and he shall give thee the desires of thine heart.

Commit thy way unto the Lord; trust also in him; and he shall bring it to pass.

And he shall bring forth thy righteousness as the light, and thy judgment as the noonday.

Psalm 37:4-6

Commit thy works unto the Lord, and thy thoughts shall be established.

Proverbs 16:3

The next morning when I woke up, I decided not to tell anybody about my experience. I thought, *Ah, you went to church last night and got kicked out. You thought you saw God. You got all emotional. Man, just forget it. It was just some weird thing that happened to you. Don't tell anybody about it. Everybody will think that you've gone nuts, so just keep it to yourself.*

I called Reeni in Ohio and told her that I missed her so much and that I needed her to come out on the road with me. To my surprise, she said, "Yes, I'll fly to San Diego and meet you."

Several days later, I went out to the airport to meet her. When she walked down off the plane, she looked gorgeous. She was wearing a little short skirt and a pair of high heels. She was all decked out, her hair was beautiful, she was smiling, she seemed so happy. I thought, *I have never seen her look as happy as she does right now. I figured, Man, she has really missed me.*

She came running to me, threw her arms around me, gave me a big kiss and then said to me, "Praise the Lord, Jeff! I've been born again! I've received Jesus as my Lord and Savior!"

I buried my face in my hands and moaned, "Oh no, not you."

She then went on to tell me that the only reason she had agreed to come to San Diego was to inform me that she had been born again and that she loved me and wanted to marry me. I immediately realized that she had not decided to party with me and give up her virtuous ways, but rather quite the contrary. If anything, she had gotten "worse." She told me that she was in love with me but that she wouldn't go on the road with me. She would not live with me but she, in fact, wanted to marry me, and be my wife.

I thought, *You've got to be kidding!* (It was lucky for me that Reeni hadn't read the Scripture that says Christians are not to be unequally yoked!)

Be ye not unequally yoked together with unbelievers: for what fellowship hath righteousness with unrighteousness? and what communion hath light with darkness?

2 Corinthians 6:14

I decided to think this thing out logically. I realized that Reeni was the most gorgeous young lady I had ever known. She was from a wealthy family and now she had become a woman of faith. I knew that she would be faithful to me and not allow herself to become involved in the type of lifestyle I led. I knew that I needed the kind of stability that she could bring to my life.

If I told her that I wouldn't marry her, I knew she would get back on that plane and I would never see her again. If I told her that I would marry her, it would buy me some time.

What the heck? I thought. *If it doesn't work, there is always divorce. If I decide I don't want her anymore after a month or two months, I can just get rid of her. Most of my friends have already been divorced once or twice, so what's the big deal?* So we began to talk marriage.

About this time, I flew up to Los Angeles to meet with the executive vice-president of CBS records. I wanted to discuss my next album. When I arrived at his office, I was told that he had been delayed several hours and that I would have to come back later.

Outside I noticed that there were thousands of long-haired heavy metal rock and roll-type people hanging around the Aquarius Theater. I went over and asked what was going on. I was told that auditions were being held for a big upcoming rock tour to be called *Jesus Christ Superstar.*

I went backstage and asked if I could audition. The manager told me, "Take a number, kid. We've got thousands of people here. We advertised an open audition in the *Los Angeles Times* and there are so many people here that it will take days before we get around to hearing you."

I thought I was the most intense singer on earth, so I just knew that I was doing these people a favor by even being there. I looked that man right in the eye and said, "Look, dude, I'm flying out of here in three hours. If you want to hear me sing, you're going to have to see me right now or you won't see me at all!"

The man disappeared into the hall. A couple of minutes later he returned and said, "All right, kid, you're on."

I walked out on that stage, picked up a guitar and started singing a song that I had written called "Hittin' the Road." When I had finished singing, Robert Stigwood, the Bee Gee's and Eric Clapton's manager and the former manager of the Beatles, came up and shook my hand, telling me, "You have one hell of a voice, kid." His assistant took my name and telephone number and I split.

Jeff on the cover of Time Magazine's October 25, 1971 issue.
Copyright © 1971 Time, Inc. reprinted by Permission.

3
Jesus Christ Superstar

Later I received a call from the people in Los Angeles. They wanted me to fly to New York and meet with some of the bigwigs there and do some more singing for them. When I got to New York, some blond-haired man met me and spoke to me in a very effeminate manner.

"I like your style, kid," he told me. "I'd like to have you over for dinner tonight."

Now I may have been born yesterday, but I was born early and I stayed up late. I immediately knew that this man was interested in more than just my voice. So I told him, "Man, I ain't interested in having dinner with you. Don't get in my face anymore. You understand?"

I went and sang for the executives at a big theater on Broadway. After my audition was over, everybody slapped me on the back and said, "Kid, you mean to say that you're only twenty years old, you sing like that and you've got all this going for you?"

I just looked at them and answered, "Yeah, yeah, I know I'm cool."

I went back to my hotel. Later I received a phone call from the yellow-haired man I had met earlier. In a very nasty tone of voice he told me, "I'm the one who's in control of everything here and I have decided that I don't want you. So you're free to go. Get back on your plane and get out of here!"

The next day I got up and left. I flew back to the West Coast. I told Reeni that I didn't get the gig, that I wasn't going to be in the production.

"Yes, you are, Jeff," she told me. "While I was praying the other night the Lord spoke to me and told me that you are going to be the lead singer in *Jesus Christ Superstar*. Nothing is going to stop you from getting that position."

I looked at her and thought, *This girl is crazy. She just wants to make a lot of money. Right now, I'm making a couple of thousand a week. She knows if I get mixed in with the Beatles' manager and those other people, I'm going to be making tons of bucks. So she's just excited.*

Two days later the telephone rang and a man with an English accent started screaming on the other end of the line, "Is this Jeffrey Fenholt?"

"Yes, it is," I replied.

"God, lad," he blurted out, "we have been searching all over the earth for you. Why did you leave New York?"

"Well, some man called me and told me that you didn't want me there, so I left."

"Well, let me assure you that whoever that man is he will be fired immediately. We do want you and are asking that you fly here to New York right away. You are to sing the lead part of Jesus in our production of *Jesus Christ Superstar*."

Reeni and I got on an airplane and flew to New York. When we arrived, there was a limousine waiting for us at the airport. We were put up in the St. Moritz Hotel, which is where the wealthiest of the wealthy stay. I began to realize that this *Jesus Christ Superstar* was definitely going to be a big event.

I began working with Andrew Lloyd Webber, the composer of *Superstar.* I liked him very much. I went into rehearsals with the band; a full orchestra was added later. Peter Brown, former Beatles' manager and President of the Robert Stigwood Organization, signed me to a personal management agreement. They renegotiated and greatly increased the advance on my CBS contract.

The album of *Jesus Christ Superstar* immediately sold six million double albums. Then it went to eight million, and then to twelve million and so on.

We opened in Pittsburgh at the arena and drew a capacity crowd of some twenty thousand screaming fans. The tour went on from there. We were performing as a basic rock group with orchestra. I wore blue jeans, silk shirts and gold jewelry. I shook my long hair and just screamed at the audience. I figured, *What the heck? I come out here for two hours a night and sing about this* Jesus Christ Superstar *thing, and we bring in three hundred thousand dollars a night. Man, this is it! We're happening now!*

I was scheduled to do a gig in Chattanooga, Tennessee, so Reeni and I flew on ahead and got married. It was worth the trip.

Robert Stigwood flew us to New York City. He told me that management had decided to take the production to Broadway in several months and that they wanted me to open as Jesus. I agreed to do it.

Jesus Christ Superstar became so bizarre. We were performing to bomb threats. There were people trying to shoot me in different cities, so I had to be constantly surrounded by security forces. The Beatles' management said they had not seen anything like it since the Beatles' tour in the mid-sixties. It was total lunacy. I believed that everybody around me wanted to shoot me or to save me, and I wasn't particularly interested in either.

One night at the Boston Gardens I was backstage getting ready to go on and perform. All of a sudden a presence came on me that I can't explain. I can only say that it was the most horrible feeling I had ever experienced in my life. Something supernatural took hold of me, and it was not the Spirit of the Lord.

I went on stage and when I stood before the crowd they began cheering and screaming. Their applause sounded like the roar of a lion. A demonic voice spoke to me and said, "You are the lion tamer and the audience is your lion! Crack your whip and they will jump through the hoop! I will give you wealth and power and fame, but you must bow down to me."

> ...the devil taketh him [Jesus] up into an exceeding high mountain, and sheweth him all the kingdoms of the world, and the glory of them;
>
> And saith unto him, All these things will I give thee, if thou wilt fall down and worship me.
>
> Matthew 4:8,9

After that incident I became so paranoid that I could barely function. From that point on, I was constantly hearing voices. I began speaking in strange languages when I would go into a trance-like state. Satan has a counterfeit for everything, and, yes, he does have a counterfeit of the gift of tongues:

> For what I do, that I will do, that I may cut off occasion from them which desire occasion; that wherein they glory, they may be found even as we.
>
> For such are false apostles, deceitful workers, transforming themselves into the apostles of Christ.
>
> And no marvel; for Satan himself is transformed into an angel of light.
>
> Therefore it is no great thing if his ministers also be transformed as the ministers of righteousness; whose end shall be according to their works.
>
> **2 Corinthians 11:12-15**

It is impossible to call upon the name of the Lord Jesus Christ and receive demonic tongues. However, I was not calling on the name of the Lord, and I had become demon-possessed.

> And there was in their synagogue a man with an unclean spirit; and he cried out.
>
> **Mark 1:23**

Many of the big rock and roll people were coming out on the tour to visit us. I met members of the Rolling Stones, Led Zeppelin, Bad Company, Pink Floyd, Eric Clapton and many other rock groups and stars. I was making television appearances and socializing with such Hollywood celebrities as Henry "Hank" Fonda, Desi Arnaz Jr. and Sr., Lauren Bacall, Diana Ross, Liza Minnelli and others. I was hanging around with the "king pins," the superstars of the entertainment industry.

When I arrived in New York City to begin rehearsals for the Broadway opening, pandemonium broke out. We had the largest advance ticket sales of any show in the history of Broadway. We were bringing in more money than any other venture in the music industry.

Every place I went, there were cameras snapping my picture.

We rehearsed for six weeks and then opened to an astounding crowd. Everyone, from Jackie Onassis to White House staff to former Beatle members, was in the audience. Later that night, we threw a party at Tavern on the Green. Tennessee Williams, Natalie Wood and some of the biggest celebrities in the world attended. That evening John Lennon spoke these words: "Rock and roll finally has class, mate! We're on Broadway!" That week I was on the cover of *Time Magazine*.

Reeni began socializing with musicians' wives. Then she found a fellowship of believers in New York City and started attending Bible studies. I figured, *There she goes again, totally nuts!* Much to my surprise, a lady who was one of the Vanderbilts was born again and Reeni began socializing with a very wealthy group of Christians. They kept inviting me to come to their Bible studies, but I would say, "No way, no way, get lost."

The pressure of doing Broadway was amazingly intense. Night after night I felt the spiritual weight of performing the role of Jesus, and I got to the place where I didn't even want to hear His name mentioned. I didn't want to know what anybody thought of Him. I didn't want to know whether He was God or a prophet. I didn't want to know anything about Him. I just wanted to be left completely alone. I wanted to be stoned, to be drunk. I wanted to hang out with young ladies and rock and rollers. That was my life: drugs, sex and rock music.

Reeni and I spent weekends in a sixteen-bedroom South Hampton home. I bought my first new car, a

Mercedes limousine. Needless to say, our lifestyle had changed dramatically.

I continued to perform on Broadway, eight shows a week, for approximately two years. One night backstage I felt as though I had the flu. I began to get sick and vomit. I was shocked to see that I was vomiting bright red blood. It was coming out my nose and mouth. I called Reeni and told her what was happening. She phoned my physician who was aware of my drug and drinking problem. He told me that I needed to get in a cab, not wait for an ambulance, and get to the New York University Hospital immediately.

When I arrived at the hospital, the medical staff stuck needles in my arms and began administering blood transfusions. They discovered that I had only two pints of blood in my entire body. Dr. Lindner stated at the time that he had never seen anyone alive with only two pints of blood in his body, let alone walking into a hospital under his own power.

I spent several weeks in the hospital and when I was released I refused to go back to the show. The management had trouble finding someone who could sing the part of Jesus night after night. Eventually the show was closed.

I moved out to Long Island and bought a huge estate in Belle Terre, New York. We kept our place in New York City and I frequently lived in Salvador Dali's castle in Spain, which had been built in 1054 A.D. Dali and his wife, Gala, were our closest friends at the time. I decided that I had been working on the road and performing so long it was time for a rest.

I left CBS and signed with Capitol Records. I went from the Robert Stigwood organization to Joe Greenburg of Alive Entertainment, who managed rock star Alice Cooper. Then I went from their management to Bruce Payne, who managed Deep Purple, and I signed with Polygram Records.

During this period of time I was recording albums off and on, but was not really very interested in my career. I was more interested in living the fast life of a wealthy young rock star. I drove fast cars and lived in the so-called fast lane. I learned that if you are going to live in the fast lane, you had better check the exit signs!

> **For what is a man profited, if he shall gain the whole world, and lose his own soul? or what shall a man give in exchange for his soul?**
>
> **Matthew 16:26**

Reeni began noticing that I was getting deeper and deeper into drugs and more and more involved in the occult. I was going to parties with satanists and hanging out with people who conjured demons. Many people will still challenge the fact that there is satanism in the heavy rock scene. I'm here to tell you that satanism runs long, hard and deep and is the basic undergirding of all rock music.

Many successful musicians, rock groups, and management organizations that I encountered were involved in satanism, the occult or the so-called New Age Movement. This is not a coincidence!

I don't believe that music is itself demonic simply because of its sound, but I do believe that when the

Jeff in front of his <u>Van Gelderan</u> painting and decapitated Jesus.

Jeff rocks in concert.

All dressed up and going to Hell.

The castle of Jeff's best friend — the famous artist Salvador Dali.
Jeff lived here in Spain several months out of the year for 10 years.

4
Spiritual Warfare

Reeni began witnessing to me more and more, and eventually I got to the place where I couldn't stand listening to her talk about God.

One night I attacked her in the entrance foyer of our mansion. I beat her the way a man would go after another man if he were trying to kill him. I left her lying unconscious on the dining room floor. I took all the flowers out of the vase in the foyer and dumped the water in her face, but she still didn't move. I realized that she was very badly hurt, but I was too drunk and demonic to care. I climbed the stairs and went to bed.

The next day I woke up and Reeni was gone. I began calling around to her friends asking them if they were hiding her out. I knew that many of the people around her, especially the Christians, were concerned about her living with someone as violent and full of hatred as I was.

I phoned one of her girlfriends and asked, "Is Reeni there with you?"

"No, you fool," she answered, "Reeni is in the hospital. She could die, and we are seeing if we can get you charged with assault and attempted murder."

I immediately hung up the receiver and freaked!

I had beaten Reeni so badly on her back that I had bruised her kidneys. Her fever was 105 degrees and there was a good chance that she would not survive.

I rushed to the airport, caught a plane and flew to Barcelona, Spain. I then disappeared by staying in the castle in the countryside of Gerona.

Two or three weeks later I learned that Reeni had, in fact, survived my savage attack. I then flew back to New York and occupied my mansion.

I was served with papers and told that I had to appear in court, that my wife had filed for a legal separation. She wanted the house and a substantial amount of my estate and was seeking an order of protection.

The day of the court hearing arrived. I looked at Reeni in the hallway before we went into court and I was physically attracted to her. I thought, *This woman is gorgeous. She is so pretty all dressed up in that beautiful silk dress. Man, I need this woman back.*

No, I didn't love her the way a man is supposed to love a woman. I loved her physically. I looked upon her in a very fleshly, worldly way. But nevertheless I decided that I was going to try to win her over before we went into the courtroom.

So I walked over to her and said, "Hey, baby, I'm your man and I know you still love me 'cause if you didn't you would be filing for divorce."

She looked at me and said, "Wait a minute, I would love to divorce you. I'm not going to take a beating from you or anybody else. God has not called me to be a punching bag. I would love nothing better than to divorce you and leave you completely, but I have been praying for you and God has spoken to me. He has told me that you are going to be saved and filled with the Holy Spirit, so I am not permitted to divorce you."

Now that blew my mind. Reeni's attorney leaned over and spoke to me as well. He said, "I'm praying for you too." I looked at them and asked, "What are you two, a team?"

My attorney, who was a Jewish friend of mine, went over to Reeni and said, "I hope you like that Gucci coat you're wearing because it's the last one you're ever going to have. I hope you enjoyed your charge accounts and your Mercedes convertibles because you won't be driving those cars or using those charge accounts anymore. Everything stops. Your money flow ends today."

Reeni's attorney told my lawyer, "Stop threatening my client." And then the two attorneys got into an argument.

I got more and more nervous and went over to the drinking fountain and took a couple more Valium capsules and a Percodan. My attorney said to me, "Keep your mouth shut. When we enter the courtroom, don't say a word. I'm going to question Maureen. I'm going to level the charge of mental cruelty. I'm going to make her out to be the fanatic and lunatic that she is. I'm going to ask her about that strange language she prays in. I'm going to ask her about her Bible groups. I'm going to ask her about the times that she has done so-called spiritual warfare in your house and all the other stuff.

Don't worry. I'm going to make a fool out of that girl. She's a religious fanatic. I'm going to show that to the judge who, by the way, also happens to be Jewish."

When we got into the courtroom, I was so ripped out of my mind I don't remember what happened. All I do know is that for some reason I decided that I was going to yell at the judge.

Let me explain something to you. If you are ever facing a judge, take my advice, *don't yell at him!*

The judge immediately ruled in Reeni's favor. Then he explained to me what the term "community property" means. In my case it meant that Reeni got all the property and I had to get out of the community.

> Because he hath set his love upon me, therefore will I deliver him: I will set him on high, because he hath known my name.
>
> Psalm 91:14
>
> Deliver me, O Lord, from the evil man: preserve me from the violent man.
>
> Psalm 140:1
>
> No weapon that is formed against thee shall prosper; and every tongue that shall rise against thee in judgment thou shalt condemn. This is the heritage of the servants of the Lord, and their righteousness is of me, saith the Lord.
>
> Isaiah 54:17

God delivered and protected Reeni. I was out of the house for approximately eight months. During that time I stayed on a continuous drunken, drugged-out binge.

I began calling Reeni and asking her if she would get together with me. She told me that the only way she would see me was in a public place, such as a restaurant or park, someplace where there were lots of people. She was afraid of me and she didn't want me getting violent with her anymore. I convinced her, over a period of time, that I had changed. I told her that if she would let me come back to the house I would live as her husband and would change my ways. Reeni was in love with me. And, of course, you can't blame her. I was such a wonderful person and had always treated her so well! Eventually, despite my violent nature and past faults, she agreed to let me come home.

Two days after I had come home I cornered Reeni upstairs in the library. I was drunk and had taken some cocaine and was full of the devil. I looked at her with hatred and I yelled, "I am going to kill you, woman! Yeah, you've got an order of protection. Maybe I'm going to jail, but you're going to be dead!"

Then a very strange thing happened. Reeni turned her little 5'6", 105-pound frame toward me, pointed her tiny finger in my face and screamed at the top of her lungs, "I bind you, Satan, in the name of Jesus!"

All of a sudden my mind became clear, perfectly clear. I looked at her and said, "You what?"

"I bind you, Satan, in the name of Jesus. Get thee behind me, Satan, for it is written, thou shalt worship the Lord thy God and serve Him only. Every knee shall bow and every tongue confess that Jesus Christ is Lord. Greater is He Who is in me than he who is in the world. Jesus Who is with me is greater than the devil who is with you, and I bind you, Satan, in the name of Jesus. The Lord rebuke you. Depart from me now."

I was stunned.

"You what?" I asked. "You bind Satan? You're pointing at me and binding Satan? Maureen, you're hallucinating. You think I'm Satan? What do you see, horns? Baby, what do I have, a pointed tail all of a sudden? You are nuts. You are emotionally and mentally disturbed. You are a sick woman, Maureen, and I ain't going to beat up no sick woman!"

And I left.

That was all Reeni needed to hear and see. From that point on, she made my life miserable. She bound every spirit from here to Burma! Every time I came in the house she was binding demons, binding the devil, binding this, binding that. I kept thinking, *This woman is sick.* Every time she would bind a demon, I would feel as if I was going to throw up and I would have to leave the room.

One day I came home with a bass player from a large rock group, a buddy of mine. We had been out drinking together. When we came in the house Reeni was having a Bible study group. I yelled through the French doors into the living room, "Hey, pretty ladies, you want to party with the bad boys?"

Reeni stood up in the middle of that group and screamed out, "I bind you...!" And I yelled back, "We're leaving!"

When we got outside, my buddy said to me, "My God, Jeff, you almost ran over me getting out of the house. What's the matter with you? It made me nervous too, but you almost knocked me down."

"Well, let me explain something to you," I told him. "I have had to think about this. I have noticed that every time my wife yells at me, I do leave. You see, my wife's emotionally disturbed. She's sick. She's mentally ill. I beat her up sometimes and I think I must have knocked something loose. Something's totally wrong with this woman. I can be with her at home or out in public, you know, going to a movie or out to dinner, and everything is fine. But every once in a while she starts to hallucinate. She thinks I'm Satan. And when she does that, this feeling comes over me like I'm going to throw up because I can't stand to be around mentally ill people. So I just have to run. That's what it is."

I would go to sleep at night and wake up the next morning with grease all over my head. I keep thinking, *What is this? Why does this woman keep pouring oil on me in the middle of the night?* I would ask her, "Is this another symptom of your disease, woman? What's with you? Are you cooking in bed? Why do you keep pouring oil on my head while I'm asleep? It's a good thing you're so gorgeous, because you're crazy — and *ugly* and crazy I could never deal with!"

Then Reeni started throwing out all of my rude magazines. She even threw away some of my gold jewelry that had certain "symbols" on it. She continued doing what she called "spiritual cleaning" in the house, inviting her girlfriends to come help her. They would go through the house doing "spiritual warfare." They would actually be raising their hands in the air!

I asked Reeni, "What are you women doing? You look like you've got a little train going through here or something. What is this?"

"Oh, we're doing a spiritual cleaning, honey," she told me, "don't worry."

"What are you spiritually cleaning? Have you got a spiritual broom?" Then I concluded, "You ladies are nuts!"

She even started bringing grandmothers into the house to help her. I used to curse Reeni's girlfriends, but how can you cuss out a little white-haired grand-motherly type who tells you she loves you and that Jesus loves you too?

I remember one day when my accountant freaked out. He came to me and asked, "Are you aware that your wife is writing checks for thousands upon thousands of dollars to Christian organizations?"

"Look, man, I spend my money on good stuff; you know: cars, booze and women," I told him. "If my wife wants to waste her fun money on those Christians, that's her business. She's crazy, but let her do it."

So everybody around me started realizing that my wife was nuts.

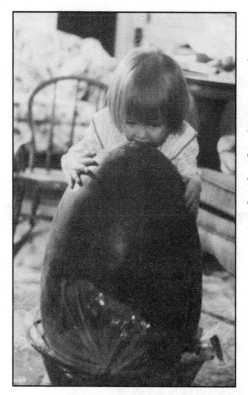

A gift from Salvador and Gala Dali to daughter Shaye — a jeweled Fabergé egg with a 100 lb. chocolate Easter Egg inside.

Reeni in front of our 1800's historical, colonial weekend home.

Reeni usually wore sunglasses indoors to hide the bruises.

Shaye with her dog Jeff beat to death.

5

Redeemed, Revived, Restored

One day I came home from Europe. As I was pulling down the long driveway in my limousine, my driver, whom I used to refer to as "The Grump," pointed at the back of the driveway servants' entrance and started laughing.

"What's so funny?" I asked.

"Remember how your wife was saying that she wanted to remodel a wing of this estate?"

"Yeah."

"Well, look at the pickup trucks over there; they've got Jesus stickers all over them. Reeni's having a revival!"

And he laughed uproariously. I thought, *Man, in the eight years he has been my driver, I've never heard The Grump laugh once, and now he's absolutely howling.*

So I got out of the car and went into the house thinking, *I'm going to tell this bunch of sissies off.* I walked in, pushed open the door and started yelling at Reeni.

"We need to get rid of these guys!" I shouted.

"If you want to get rid of them, go right ahead," she answered.

For some reason, I was afraid to enter the part of the house where the men were working. So I went and got drunk and stayed away the rest of the day.

The next morning I woke up at "the crack of noon," and went downstairs to face those guys.

Now, at that time, there was a preacher on television who was based somewhere in the Northeast and who looked like a cue ball with a rug on top. He spoke like the Munchkins from the Wizard of Oz. He sounded like a sissy on "acid." I can remember him saying, "If you'll just send in your money, we'll have Miss Lucy pray for you and we'll just believe that everything is going to be fine in your life."

I thought, *All these guys are after is money. They're all just a bunch of sissies. I don't want to have anything to do with them.*

I imagined that these Christian carpenters Reeni had brought in were probably all wearing darling little elf outfits and sweetly tapping away with their little hammers like the Seven Dwarfs. So I figured I would walk through the door and they would look up at me with their dainty little eyes sparkling, and in some effeminate manner say something like, "O joyous day! How art thou, friend?"

Instead I pushed open the door and there before my astonished eyes were ten bulky men in ripped-off T-shirts with tatoos all over their arms. Some of them had long hair. One had a beard hanging down his chest. Another had his hair greased back. One sported a butch hairdo.

"My God," I blurted out. "You guys aren't Christians! You're too ugly to be Christians! You look like "roadies"!"

"Yeah, we are, we're Christians. Some of us have only been saved a few weeks, but we love the Lord Jesus Christ. We were drug addicts, living on the streets of New York. Then Nick DiSipio came down with some men and witnessed to us, laid hands on us in Jesus' name and delivered us from drugs. Now we're working for his construction company. We're earning money to pay for a big ranch so all us guys who have been delivered from drugs will have a place to live till we hit the streets again for the glory of God."

I thought, *Man, these guys are nuts. Are you kidding me? You mean these roughneck dudes are allowed to be into Jesus?* I had never heard of such a thing. So I decided I wouldn't talk to them. I said, "I want to talk to Nick DiSipio, the chief contractor."

Around the corner came this fat Italian man, standing about five-eight and weighing about 250 pounds. He had his hair greased back and was holding a hammer in his pudgy hands. As it turns out, Nick DiSipio had been saved out of the Mafia. He had grown up in Italy and spoke with a very strong Italian accent.

I looked at him and asked, "You're Nick DiSipio?"

"That's a'right."

"Well, I want to talk to you, man."

He walked toward me, jabbed his finger right in my face and said, "No, I wanna talk'a to you. You're some'a big'a rock star; you played the part of Jesus a'Christ

Superstar. Now, are you ready to meet the real Jesus a'Christ?"

"No," I said. "You've got a lot of nerve coming in here trying to talk to me, Bozo. Nobody asked you nothin' about Jesus a'Christ. Get out of my face."

Then Nick DiSipio motioned to his crew and said, "Come here, men. We're a'gonna pray for this a'man."

I said, "Don't pray for me. Pray for your mama. You know what your mama is? Your mama's a whore!"

Nick was obviously wearing the full armor of God because he did not flinch.

> Finally, my brethren, be strong in the Lord, and in the power of his might.
>
> Put on the whole armour of God, that ye may be able to stand against the wiles of the devil.
>
> For we wrestle not against flesh and blood, but against principalities, against powers, against the rulers of the darkness of this world, against spiritual wickedness in high places.
>
> Wherefore take unto you the whole armour of God, that ye may be able to withstand in the evil day, and having done all, to stand.
>
> Ephesians 6:10-13

You have to know that there was a heavy demonic activity going on in my life. For a skinny little 128-pound, long-haired rock and roller to yell in the face of an ex-Mafia Italian construction worker, telling him that his mother was a whore, is a sure sign that something was going on that was not right.

I even spit at Nick DiSipio. I told him that I had a limousine driver outside waiting for me who was packing a .38-caliber revolver and that if anybody touched me I would have him killed. I warned the crew that they were on my property and that I had a right to have them shot.

Nick DiSipio yelled at the top of his lungs, "You go get'a your limousine driver!"

"Yeah?" I asked. "You want to see Uncle a'Knuckles and his'a .38, do you?"

"Yes," said Nick. "Go get him and tell'a him to come in here. If he can get'a past the blood of Jesus a'Christ, you tell Uncle a'Knuckles to be my guest. Bring him in. We'll pray for him'a, too."

Nick had no fear.

Ye are of God, little children, and have overcome them: because greater is he that is in you, than he that is in the world.

They are of the world: therefore speak they of the world, and the world heareth them.

We are of God: he that knoweth God heareth us; he that is not of God heareth not us. Hereby know we the spirit of truth, and the spirit of error.

1 John 4:4-6

I realized then that nothing intimidated these guys. I turned around, ran out of room and rushed upstairs where I locked myself in the master bedroom. I got down on my knees and started shaking. I thought, *Man, I need some drugs.* I got up and went into the bathroom. As I was taking the drugs out of the medicine cabinet, a voice spoke to me. At that point I knew that I was right in the heat of spiritual warfare. I thought then that it was the Lord Who was speaking to me saying, "Go ahead, you do need drugs." It startled me. I put the drugs back, even though I thought that was what I needed.

I look back now and I see that the voice was that of an evil spirit who was trying to finish me off. I was so confused and in such panic, I didn't know who was talking to me. I didn't know which voice was Satan's and which was God's. All I knew was that I was desperate.

...When the enemy shall come in like a flood, the spirit of the Lord shall lift up a standard against him.
Isaiah 59:19

For God is not the author of confusion, but of peace....
1 Corinthians 14:33

But if ye have bitter envying and strife in your hearts, glory not, and lie not against the truth.

This wisdom descendeth not from above, but is earthly, sensual, devilish.

For where envying and strife is, there is confusion and every evil work.

But the wisdom that is from above is first pure, then peaceable, gentle, and easy to be entreated, full of mercy and good fruits, without partiality, and without hypocrisy.

And the fruit of righteousness is sown in peace of them that make peace.
James 3:14-18

Then I thought, *I need some whiskey. I've got to go downstairs to get some liquor. I need something bad. I'm hearing voices. I'm paranoid. I'm having panic attacks continuously. I always have to be drunk or stoned or in bed with some girl, constantly doing something in order to occupy my mind. If I ever let down for even a minute, I'll start to freak out. Even if I got on a rocket ship and went to the moon, I would still be paranoid. There's no place to run, nowhere to hide. I'm in for the ride.*

64

And then I began to silently scream from the depth of my soul, "I need something!"

In the last day, that great day of the feast, Jesus stood and cried, saying, If any man thirst, let him come unto me, and drink.

He that believeth on me, as the scripture hath said, out of his belly shall flow rivers of living water.

John 7:37,38

After three hours of wrestling with what I now know to be the Holy Spirit, I finally decided that I was going to go downstairs and have those men pray for me. As soon as I made the decision, a voice spoke to me from the depths of hell. A familiar spirit that had been tormenting me for years spoke up and said, "Those are not Christians. You've been in the occult, and the devil knows you are getting ready to reach out to God, so Satan has sent his men here. I am God and I am giving you a warning. Those men have been sent from the satanic church. Nobody here knows where they're from. Your wife doesn't know who they really are. Do they look like Christians to you? They have been ordered to ask you if you want to receive Jesus as Lord, and if you say yes, they have been ordered to kill you on the spot. Because you played the part of Jesus, the devil does not want to let you go."

Now, you talk about being paranoid! All I knew was that I had come to the end of my rope. I could see that I had been following a long, wide road and that now it had split, with one branch going to the right and the other to the left. One way led to heaven, one way led to hell. It was time to make a decision.

(For he saith, I have heard thee in a time accepted, and in the day of salvation have I succoured thee: behold, now is the accepted time; behold, now is the day of salvation.)

2 Corinthians 6:2

I knelt down. Even though I didn't know how to pray, I cried out, "God, Whoever You are, true God, I'm speaking to You now. If those men are satanists and I go downstairs and they kill me today, then when I come before You, I want You to remember that I died trying to find You."

I stood up, unlocked the door of my bedroom and started walking down the hall. I then proceeded down the back staircase. As I moved along I felt every muscle in my body become tight and rigid. I felt as if I needed a Quaalude or some kind of a drink to take the edge off my nerves. But I refused to give in; I just kept walking.

When I got to the back wing of the house and approached the door, I took a deep breath. I thought, *On the other side of this door is either life or death.* I then opened the door.

All the men stopped their work and stood staring at me. Nick DiSipio walked up close to me and said, "Praise a'God!" I looked at him and thought to myself, *I'm going to outsmart these guys.* I remembered what that voice had told me about their being satanists, so I told Nick DiSipio, "I'm not into Jesus and I don't want to be. But if you guys want to pray for me, go ahead and pray. Let's see Who your God is." In my heart, I silently spoke these words: *Jesus, if You are real, help me.*

Behold, I stand at the door, and knock: if any man hear my voice, and open the door, I will come in to him, and will sup with him, and he with me.

Revelation 3:20

Those men came running at me like a herd of stampeding buffaloes. They laid hands on me and began to pray. I heard these words: "I bind you, Satan, in the name of Jesus." As they spoke, a feeling of terror came over my entire being. I started to scream and I tried to run. As I turned, this big dude grabbed me, put his arm around my neck, got me in a stronghold, and said, "You ain't going nowhere, fella! Praise the Lord Jesus Christ!"

That's the last thing I remember.

The next thing I knew I was down on my knees. I went down full of hell, but within a few moments I stood up clear-minded, washed in the blood of Jesus. I looked at those men and said, "My God, something has left me, something has happened."

Nick DiSipio spoke up and asked me, "How do you feel'a now?"

I said, "I feel like my back opened up and an anvil was lifted out of the inside of my spine."

Grace be to you and peace from God the Father, and from our Lord Jesus Christ,

Who gave himself for our sins, that he might deliver us from this present evil world, according to the will of God and our Father.

Galatians 1:3,4

I looked out the window and I could actually focus on the leaves of the trees. This might sound like a small thing, but to me it was amazing; I had been blurry-eyed for ten years. I stared at those men and I started to jump up and down, leaping for joy. I began, not laughing, but giggling, like a schoolgirl. I yelled at Nick DiSipio, "What has happened? What did you do?"

"We prayed'a for you in the name of Jesus a'Christ," he answered, "and He has a'delivered you by His precious blood. He has a'delivered you out of all that'a garbage you've been into."

"If this is Jesus," I said, "I want Him right now. What do I do? I want Jesus. I want more. What do I do?"

> **For whosoever shall call upon the name of the Lord shall be saved.**
>
> **Romans 10:13**

"Pray with us," the men said, "and receive Jesus now as your personal Savior and Lord."

I got on my knees and prayed the sinner's prayer:

"Father, I come to You in the name of Jesus. I'm a sinner.

"Dear Jesus, thank You for delivering me. Thank You for setting me free. Wash me in Your precious blood. Heal me and clean me up. Make me a new person.

"Lord, I'll serve You for ever and ever. I belong to the Father, the Son and the Holy Ghost now and forevermore.

"Jesus, I praise You! Jesus, Jesus, Jesus!"

And then I said, "Amen." And all of us said, "Amen."

At that point Reeni came into the room and saw me on my knees receiving Jesus as Savior and Lord. Immediately she fell over and collapsed on the floor. I looked at her and asked, "What's the matter with Reeni?"

"Aw, it's a'nothin'," said Nick DiSipio, "she's been a'slain in the Spirit."

"Slain?"

I didn't know that the expression "slain in the Spirit" meant that the presence of God was so strong in the room that Reeni had fallen under the power of the Lord. I thought Nick meant that she was dead. I said, "Get away from her! What are you doing?"

I leaned over to Reeni and I noticed that she was mumbling in tongues. Then suddenly I realized that I too was speaking in those same tongues. I started jumping around and found myself speaking in a whole new language, the language of the Holy Spirit.

And they were all filled with the Holy Ghost, and began to speak with other tongues, as the Spirit gave them utterance.

Acts 2:4

It was bringing me joy and peace and power. My mind felt so strong and so clear. I knew that I knew that I knew that I would never need drugs or alcohol again as long as I serve the Lord Jesus Christ. I was free! I was free indeed!

For God hath not given us the spirit of fear; but of power, and of love, and of a sound mind.

2 Timothy 1:7

Therefore if any man be in Christ, he is a new creature: old things are passed away; behold, all things are become new.

2 Corinthians 5:17

Knowing this, that our old man is crucified with him, that the body of sin might be destroyed, that henceforth we should not serve sin.

For he that is dead is freed from sin.

Romans 6:6,7

The next day when I woke up, all the carpenters were there. "Let's do a Bible study," I said.

"We can't," they said. "We've got to work and earn some money to support the ranch."

"Don't worry about it," I told them. "I'll pay all you guys' salary, but you don't have to work. Just show up here from 9 A.M. till 5 P.M. We're going to sit out on my six acres of land by the ocean and we're going to study the Word of God. I want to learn about Jesus. I want to know about heaven. I want to read the Bible and learn God's Word." So, we began holding Bible studies all day long.

The men told me that I needed to be baptized with water. I figured, *Well, I've gone this far, why not?* So the very next day they began walking me down to the beach where I was going to be baptized in the Long Island Sound.

When we got to the water, there was a naked girl lying on a towel on my private beach. I thought, *Give me a break! Have I got to go out there and get baptized in front of a naked girl?* But Nick DiSipio and his men walked over to her and began praying for her. She jumped up and took off.

As I stepped into the water, much to my surprise that same familiar spirit, the voice of that demon, spoke to me again.

"Remember," it said, "I told you they were going to kill you? Well, this is it. They are going to get you under water and hold you there until you die. Then they will say that you drowned by accident, that you took your own life in the ocean!"

At first, I started to become paranoid. But then I remembered what Jesus had done for me. So silently I turned to God and prayed, *Lord, I've gone this far, and I'm going all the way.*

I walked farther into the water and as I stepped out I looked at the muscles on those big men. They waded out waist deep and then took hold of me, saying, "Hold your nose, we're going to dunk you under the water."

They put their hands on my head and started to lean me over backwards. It was then that I realized that if they tried to hold me down bent back in that position, they could easily drown me.

"Stop! Wait a minute!" I cried. "I ain't going down backwards!"

I figured that if I was going to go down in the water with those guys, I was at least going to try to keep my legs under me so I would have a fighting chance.

They dunked me under the water. I expected them to hold me down, so I shot up with my legs. I must have jumped a foot out of the water. I came up like a nuclear missile. I am probably the only guy in the history of the Gospel of Jesus Christ who was baptized forward.

All of a sudden a feeling of total joy and peace swept over me. God then spoke to me and said, "Yes, son, something did die today. The devil died in you, and now you are born of the Spirit of the Living God."

Likewise reckon ye also yourselves to be dead indeed unto sin, but alive unto God through Jesus Christ our Lord.

Romans 6:11

Receiving Jesus as my Savior and Lord is the most wonderful experience in my whole life. Praise be to the name of the Lord, the true Messiah, Jesus!

Jeff — now doing Christian Concerts.

Jeff dedicating a church for David Wilkerson in New York City at Mark Hellinger Theater — the same theater Jeff played the lead roll of Jesus in Jesus Christ Superstar and blasphemed God. It is still Time Square Church today.

Jeff and Reeni's Belle Terre home where Jeff was "born again."

*The Fenholt California home where Jeff, Reeni and
their children still reside today.*

Conclusion

The Lord is not slack concerning his promise, as some men count slackness; but is longsuffering to us-ward, not willing that any should perish, but that all should come to repentance.

2 Peter 3:9

The Bible says that God does not want anyone to die, but that people perish ...**because they received not the love of the truth, that they might be saved** (2 Thess. 2:10).

In Matthew 11:28 Jesus says, **Come unto me, all ye that labour and are heavy laden, and I will give you rest.**

For you to be saved, you must receive Jesus as Your Lord and Savior. The Word of God says that anyone who calls on the name of the Lord will be saved. (Rom. 10:13.) To receive Jesus as your personal Savior and the Lord of your life, you need only to pray this prayer:

"Dear God, Creator of the heavens and the earth, I pray to You now, and I seek Your face. I repent of my sins and turn away from wickedness.

"Jesus, I receive You now as my Lord and Savior. Save my soul. Wash me in Your blood that was shed for me on the cross.

"Holy Spirit, I welcome you now into my life.

"I am saved. I am born again of the Spirit of the Living God. I will worship the Father and the Son and the Holy Ghost forever and ever.

"In Jesus' name. Amen."

I believe it is important for you to find and join a strong Bible-believing church in your local area. If you know someone who is a born-again Christian, I would recommend that you call him or her now and tell them what has happened in your life. I am certain they will be overjoyed.

God bless you as you continue in His love.

About the Author

Jeff Fenholt starred as the original Jesus in the production *Jesus Christ Superstar*. He toured the United States and Canada appearing before crowds of up to 135 thousand people per performance. He then went on to recreate the role of Jesus opening on Broadway. Jeff recorded the lead vocal of Jesus on the original cast recording. *Jesus Christ Superstar* has sold approximately 15 million double albums in the United States. International sales have been even greater. *Jesus Christ Superstar* is the most successful rock opera in history.

Jeff's picture has appeared on the cover of *Time Magazine*, as well as other major publications. Jeff has recorded for and released albums and singles on various labels such as CBS, MCA, DECCA, Polygram, Phonogram, Capital and others.

Jeff achieved wealth and fame, yet he felt a deep emptiness inside. He made Jesus Christ his Lord and Savior, and as he will speak forth, that is the best decision he has ever made. In December of 1984, Jeff joined the rock group "Black Sabbath," he subsequently left the group in May of 1985. Jeff was no longer interested in performing in the secular world and being unequally yoked.

Since that time, Jeff has been performing as a Christian all over the world. He has performed on five-continents, in stadiums and arenas, as well as prisons and concert halls. Jeff appears nationally on his weekly television show listed in TV Guide under the title "Jeff Fenholt." His show is available to over 100 million homes in the United States, as well as via satellite throughout the world.

For concert bookings, order forms or
to contact the author, write:

Jeffrey Fenholt Outreach
P. O. Box 5000-301
Upland, California 91786

Acknowledgements

To Diana L. Windmiller, for helping me with this composition.

To Barbara Gronbach, for persevering through time-consuming research and contacting many of the people from my past, who had knowledge of or participated in the events listed in this book.

To Christopher Leeper, for his relentless support.

The Harrison House Vision

Proclaiming the truth and the power
Of the Gospel of Jesus Christ
With Excellence;

Challenging Christians to
Live victoriously,
Grow spiritually,
Know God intimately.

Trinity Broadcasting Network

An All-Christian Television Network Broadcasting the
Gospel 24 Hours a Day via Satellite, Cable TV
and Local TV Broadcast Stations

Alphabetical Directory of TBN Owned and Affiliate Stations
(•Indicates an Affiliate-owned station)

ALASKA
•Anchorage Ch. 22
NORTH POLE Ch. 4
ALABAMA
•Birmingham Ch. 51
•Decatur Ch. 22
Dothan Ch. 41
•Florence Ch. 57
•GADSDEN Ch. 60
•Huntsville Ch. 67
•MOBILE Ch. 21
•MONTGOMERY Ch. 45
Scottsboro/
Huntsville Ch. 64
Selma Ch. 52
Tuscaloosa Ch. 46
ARKANSAS
•DeQueen Ch. 8
Fayetteville Ch. 42
Ft. Smith Ch. 27
•Harrison Ch. 66
•Little Rock Ch. 33
Mountain Home Ch. 43
ARIZONA
Cottonwood Ch. 58
Flagstaff Ch. 62
Globe Ch. 63
•Lake Havasu Ch. 25
PHOENIX Ch. 21
•Safford Ch. 17
Shonto/Tonalea Ch. 38
•Sierra Vista Ch. 33
Tuscon Ch. 57
Tuscon Ch. 56
CALIFORNIA
Alturas Ch. 30
Atwater/Merced Ch. 57
Bakersfield Ch. 55
Desert Hot Sprgs. Ch. 40
Eureka Ch. 47
•Fresno Ch. 56
•FRESNO Ch. 53
Lancaster/

Palmdale Ch. 54
•Lompoc Ch. 23
Monterey Ch. 53
Palm Springs Ch. 66
Porterville/
Visalia Ch. 15
Redding Ch. 65
Sacramento Ch. 69
•SAN JOSE Ch. 65
•San Luis Obispo Ch. 36
SANTA ANA Ch. 40
Santa Barbara Ch. 15
•Santa Maria Ch. 65
Ventura Ch. 45
Victorville Ch. 33
COLORADO
•Boulder Ch. 17
•Colorado Sprgs. Ch. 43
Denver Ch. 57
Denver Ch. 47
Denver Ch. 33
Las ANimas, Ch40
Loveland Ch. 48
•Pueblo Ch. 48
DELAWARE
Dover Ch. 67
•Wilmington Ch. 26
FLORIDA
Dunedin/
Clearwater Ch. 60
Ft. Meyers Ch. 67
•FT. PIERCE Ch. 21
•Gainsville Ch. 69
•JACKSONVILLE Ch. 59
Lake City Ch. 23
•LEESBURG/
ORLANDO Ch. 55
•Melbourne Ch. 62
MIAMI Ch. 45
•Sarasota Ch. 24
Sebring/
Vero Beach Ch. 17
St. Petersburg/

Tampa Ch. 18
•Tallahassee Ch. 17
GEORGIA
Albany Ch. 23
ATLANTA Ch. 63
Augusta Ch. 65
Brunswick Ch. 33
•DALTON Ch. 23
•Hazelhurst Ch. 63
Marietta Ch. 55
Monroe Ch 67
Savannah Ch. 67
Valdosta Ch. 54
Waycross Ch. 46
HAWAII
•HONOLULU Ch. 26
•KONA Ch. 6
IDAHO
Boise Ch. 47
Pocatello 15
Twin Falls Ch. 25
ILLINOIS
•Bloomington Ch. 64
Champaign/
Decatur Ch. 29
•LaSALLE Ch. 35
•Marian Ch. 27
Palatine Ch. 36
•QUINCY Ch. 16
•Robinson Ch. 57
•Rockford Ch. 52
Sterling & Dixon Ch. 52
Waukegan Ch. 22
INDIANA
•ANGOLA/
BLOOMINGTON Ch. 42
Evansville Ch. 38
•Jeffersonville Ch. 5
Lafayette Ch. 36
Michigan City Ch. 24
Muncie Ch. 32
RICHMOND Ch. 43
Terre Haute Ch. 65

IOWA
- •Ames Ch. 52
- Cedar Rapids Ch. 61
- Davenport/
- Bettendorf Ch. 58
- •Des Moines Ch. 35
- •Iowa City Ch. 64
- •Keokuk Ch. 60
- Ottumwa Ch. 42
- Souix City Ch. 38
- Waterloo Ch. 65

KANSAS
- Junction City Ch. 25
- Manhattan Ch. 31
- Salina Ch. 15
- Topeka Ch. 21
- Wichita Ch. 59

KENTUCKY
- •Beattyville Ch. 65
- Corbin Ch. 41
- Hopkinsville Ch. 62

LOUISIANA
- Alexandria Ch. 19
- Baton Rouge Ch. 56
- •Lake Charles Ch. 51
- Mermentau Ch. 45
- Monroe Ch. 27
- New Orleans Ch. 59
- Shreveport Ch. 65

MARYLAND
- Cresaptown/
- •Bangor Ch. 17
- •Portland Ch. 18
- Presque Isle Ch. 51
- York Center Ch. 63

MAINE
- Bangor Ch. 17
- Danforth Ch. 17
- Dover-Foxcroft Ch. 19
- Medway Ch. 14
- Portland Ch. 18
- Presque Isle Ch. 51

MICHIGAN
- Detroit Ch. 66
- Grand Rapids Ch. 19
- •JACKSON Ch. 59
- •Kalamazoo Ch. 24
- •Lancing Ch. 69
- Muskegon Ch. 29
- •MUSKEGON Ch. 54
- •SAGINAW Ch. 49
- Sault Ste Marie Ch. 67

MINNESOTA
- Duluth Ch. 58
- •Fairmont Ch. 28
- Minneapolis Ch. 58

- •New Ulm Ch. 22
- Rochester Ch. 60
- St. Cloud Ch. 19
- •Wilmar Ch. 27

MISSOURI
- •Branson Ch. 25
- Columbia Ch. 56
- •Joplin Ch. 9
- Joplin Ch. 46
- •Monett Ch. 38
- •Neosho Ch. 32
- Poplar Bluff Ch. 39
- Springfield Ch. 52
- St. Charles Ch. 34
- •ST. JOSEPH Ch. 16
- St. Louis Ch. 18

MISSISSIPPI
- Biloxi Ch. 29
- •Bruce Ch. 7
- Clarksdale Ch. 31
- Columbus Ch. 25
- Greenville Ch. 33
- Grenada Ch. 25
- Jackson Ch. 56
- •Jackson Ch. 64
- McComb Ch. 36
- Natchez Ch. 58
- Pascagoula Ch. 46

MONTANA
- •Billings Ch. 14
- Great Falls Ch. 53
- Helena Ch. 41
- Kalispell Ch. 26

NORTH CAROLINA

- Charlotte Ch. 68
- •Charlotte/
- Gastonia Ch. 62
- Durham Ch. 56
- Goldsboro Ch. 59
- •GREENSBORO Ch. 61
- Raleigh Ch. 38
- Statesville Ch. 66
- Wilmington Ch. 20

NORTH DAKOTA
- Fargo Ch. 56
- Grand Forks Ch. 22
- •Rugby Ch. 20
- Williston Ch. 40

NEBRASKA
- •Council Bluffs/
- Lincoln Ch. 39
- Ogallala Ch. 26

NEW JERSEY
- Atlantic City Ch. 36
- Cape May/

- Wildwood Ch. 5

NEW MEXICO
- •Alamogordo Ch. 29
- •ALBQUERQUE Ch. 23
- •Carlsbad Ch. 63
- •Clovis/Hobbs Ch. 65
- •Farmington Ch. 47
- Hobbs Ch. 18
- MalJamar Ch. 46
- Raton Ch. 18
- •Roswell Ch. 27
- Ruidoso Ch. 45

NEVADA
- Carson City Ch. 19
- Las Vegas Ch. 57
- Reno Ch. 45

NEW YORK
- Albany Ch. 64
- Binghampton Ch. 14
- •BUFFALO Ch. 45
- Glens Falls Ch. 14
- Jamestown Ch. 10
- •Massena Ch. 20
- Olean Ch. 22
- POUGHKEEPSIE Ch. 54
- •Rochester Ch. 59
- Utica Ch. 41

OHIO
- CANTON Ch. 17
- Chillicothe Ch. 40
- •Columbus Ch. 24
- Dayton Ch. 68
- Lexington Ch. 32
- •Marietta Ch. 26
- •Marion Ch. 39
- Portsmouth Ch. 21
- •SANDUSKY Ch. 52
- •Seaman Ch. 17
- Springfield Ch. 47
- •Toledo (North) Ch. 68
- •Toledo (South) Ch. 46
- Youngstown Ch. 39
- Zanesville Ch. 36

OKLAHOMA
- Ardmore Ch. 44
- Balko Ch. 25
- •BARTLESVILE Ch. 17
- •Guymon Ch. 53
- Lawton Ch. 27
- OKLAHOMA CTY Ch. 14

OREGON
- Bend Ch. 33
- Coos Bay Ch. 33
- Cotton Grove Ch. 50
- •Eugene Ch. 59
- Grants Pass Ch. 59

Klamath Falls Ch. 58
Lakeview Ch. 21
Medford Ch. 57
•PORTLAND Ch. 24
Roseburg Ch. 14
PENNSYLVANIA
Erie Ch. 44
•Kingston Ch. 54
Meadville Ch. 52
State College Ch. 42
Williamsport Ch. 11
SOUTH CAROLINA
Anderson Ch. 18
Charleston Ch. 44
•GREENSVILLE Ch. 16
•Greenville Ch. 58
Myrtle Beach Ch. 66
Myrtle Beach Ch. 43
SOUTH DAKOTA
Aberdeen Ch. 20
Arlington/Huron Ch. 38
Brookings Ch. 15
Huron Ch. 38
Madison Ch. 27
Rapid City Ch. 33
Sioux Falls Ch. 52
Sioux Falls/
Rowena Ch. 51
Yankton Ch. 31
TENNESSEE
•Chattanooga Ch. 23
Cookeville Ch. 46
Farragut Ch. 66
•Greenfield Ch. 2
Jackson Ch. 35
•Memphis Ch. 65
Memphis Ch. 40
Morristown Ch. 31
•Nashville Ch. 36
•NASHVILLE Ch. 50
TEXAS
Abilene Ch. 51
Austin Ch. 63
•BEAUMONT Ch. 34
Brownwood Ch. 26
College Station Ch. 57
DALLAS Ch. 58
•HARLINGEN Ch. 44
•HOUSTON Ch. 14
•Kerrville Ch. 2
•Killeen Ch. 31
Longview Ch. 10
•Lufkin Ch. 5
•ODESSA Ch. 42
Palestine Ch. 17
Paris Ch. 42

San Angelo Ch. 19
San Antonio Ch 33
San Antonio Ch20
Texarkana Ch. 8
Texarkana Ch. 30
Uvalde Ch. 15
Victoria Ch. 43
•Wichita Falls Ch. 26
UTAH
Ogden Ch. 64
•Salt Lake City Ch. 36
Vernal Ch. 39
VIRGINIA
•Danville Ch. 18
Front Royal/Winchester Ch 28
•Harrisonburg Ch. 24
Lynchburg Ch. 32
Norfolk Ch. 24
•Richmond Ch. 67
Roanoke Ch. 49
•Woodstock Ch. 10
VERMONT
Burlington Ch. 16
WASHINGTON
Aberdeen Ch. 23
Longview Ch. 36
•Richland Ch. 49
SEATTLE/
TACOMA Ch. 20
Spokane Ch. 55
•WENATCHEE Ch. 27
Wenatchee Ch 13
Wenatchee Ch 59
•Yakima Ch. 64
WISCONSIN
Green Bay Ch. 68
Janesville Ch. 19
•LaCross Ch. 44
Madison Ch. 33
Ripon Ch. 42
Sheboygan Ch. 20
Waupaca Ch. 55
WEST VIRGINIA
•Charleston Ch. 45
•Huntington Ch. 19
Parkersburg Ch. 39
WYOMING
•Casper Ch. 13
Green River Ch. 35

TBN
RADIO STATIONS :

KTBN SUPERPOWER
SHORTWAVE RADIO
8 A.M. - 6 P.M. (P.D.T.)
15.590 MHz.
6 P.M. - 8 A.M. (P.D.T.)
7.510 MHz.
(Reaching Around the World)

RADIO PARADISE
ST. KITTS, WEST
INDIES
830 KHz. A.M.

HOQUIAM, WA
KGHO AM 1490
KGHO FM 95.3

INTERNATIONAL STATIONS

NEVIS, W.I.
Charlestown Ch. 13
•GRAND CAYMAN IS.
Georgetown Ch. 21
•HAITI
Port-au-Prince Ch. 16
ST. LUCIA
Castries Ch. 13
•BELIZE
Belize City Ch. 13
•COSTA RICA
•San Jose Ch. 23
•Santa Elena Ch. 53
•Limon Ch. 23
•Cerro de la Muerte Ch. 53
EL SALVADOR
San Salvador Ch. 25
•HONDURAS
•Tegulcigalpa Ch. 57
NICARAGUA
•Managua Ch. 21
•Quiabu Ch. 15
•La Gateda Ch. 27
•ARGENTINA
•Buenos Aires Ch. 66
•BOLIVIA
• La Paz Ch. 27
CHILE
Valpariso Ch. 32
ITALY
Milano Ch. 11

Porto Ceresio Ch. 46
Como Ch. 39
Varese Ch. 33
Ponte Tresa Ch. 39
Luino Ch. 44
Nosate Ch. 41
Novara Ch. 59
Ivrea Ch. 36
Biella Ch. 59
Borgo Franco Ch. 28
Castletto Crvo. Ch. 28
  & 68
Pavia Certosa Ch. 41
SWITZERLAND
Locarno Ch. 37
Lugano/Campione Ch. 44
GREECE

Athens Ch. 62
Corinth Ch. 54
Macedonia Ch. 62
•ALBANIA (gov't. owned)
•ICELAND
•Reykjavik Ch. 45 & 53
RUSSIA
St. Petersburg Ch. 40
CISKEI, S. AFRICA
Bisho Ch. 24
TRANSKEI, S. AFRICA
Umtata Ch. 67
Butterworth Ch. 25
Ngangelizwe Ch. 67
Mt. Ayliff Ch. 27
Queenstown (under const.)
Port St. Johns (under
const.)

Engcobo (under const.)
Mt. Fletcher (under const.)
•ZAMBIA
•Lusaka
•SWAZILAND
•Mbabane
•NAMIBIA
•Windhoef
•LESOTHO
•Maseru
•BOPHUTHATSWANA
•ZAIRE
•Kinshasa
•REPUBLIC OF SOUTH
  AFRICA (SABC)
•TV 1 - Ch. 13
•TV 2 - Ch. 9

For more information, please write:
TBN
PO Box A
Santa Ana, CA 92711
24-Hour Prayer Line: (714) 731-1000